# AMAZING MOTORCYCLES

by Frances Ridley

NEW FOREST PRESS

# Contents

Words in **bold** are explained in the glossary.

North American edition copyright © TickTock Entertainment Ltd. 2010
First published in North America in 2010 by New Forest Press,
PO Box 784, Mankato, MN 56002
www.newforestpress.com

**We would like to thank: Penny Worms, Alix Wood, and the National Literacy Trust.**

ISBN 978-1-84898-381-6
Library of Congress Control Number: 2010925596  Tracking number: nfp0008
Printed in the USA
1 3 5 7 9 10 8 6 4 2

Picture credits: b=bottom; c=center; t=top; r=right; l=left
All images Car Photo Library—www.carphoto.co.uk, except: Action Plus: 15tr, 21tr;
Alvey and Towers: 20-21c, b/c cl

Every effort has been made to trace the copyright holders, and we apologize in advance for any unintentional omissions. We would be pleased to insert the appropriate acknowledgments in any subsequent edition of this publication.

# Aprilia RSV Mille R

The RSV Mille R was launched in 2002. The R stands for "Racing."

The Mille R is big, fast, and comfortable. It has a top speed of 168 mph.

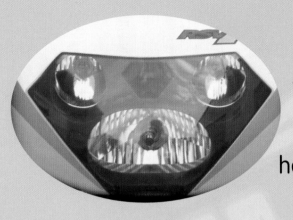

The Mille R has a triple headlight.

It also has special brakes at the front. You can stop very quickly if you need to.

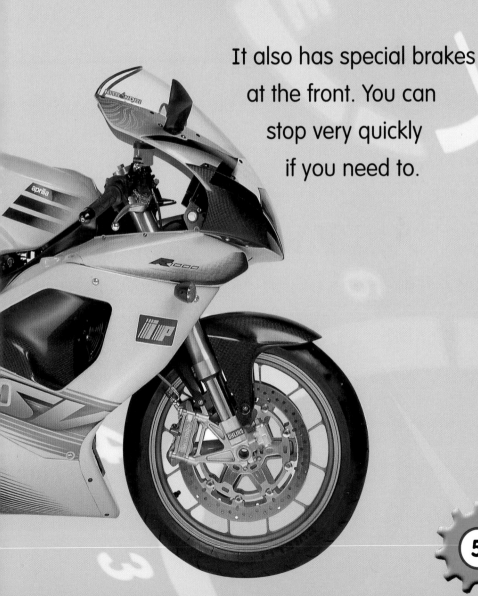

# Buell XB9R Firebolt

The Firebolt is very light for a motorbike—it only weighs 386 pounds.

Its powerful engine makes it very fast. It has a top speed of 130 mph.

The Firebolt is an unusual
bike. It has a hollow
frame to store fuel.

Its **exhaust**
is underneath
the bike, not on
the side.

# Honda CBR1100XX Blackbird

The Blackbird has a huge engine. It also has a **streamlined** shape.

It can **accelerate** from 0 to 130 mph in just 11 seconds.

In 2001, a **turbo-charged** Blackbird did a wheelie at 199 mph!

It has special brakes. They slow down the front and back tires at the same time.

# Kawasaki Ninja ZX-12R

The Ninja ZX-12R has a top speed of 190 mph. Its streamlined shape helps the bike go fast.

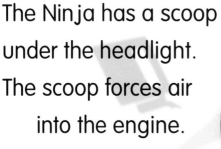

The Ninja has a scoop
under the headlight.
The scoop forces air
into the engine.

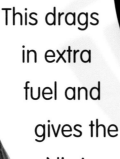

This drags
in extra
fuel and
gives the
Ninja more power.

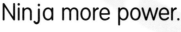

The big gas tank
lets you travel
a long way
before you need
more fuel.

# Harley-Davidson V-Rod

Harley-Davidson launched the V-Rod in 2002. It's much lighter and faster than other Harley-Davidson bikes.

The V-Rod's fuel tank is under the seat. This leaves room for air intakes, giving the V-Rod more power.

This badge shows that Harley-Davidson has made bikes since 1903.

# Ducati 999S

There are three kinds of Ducati 999. The 999S has a top speed of over 170 mph and can accelerate from 0 to 62 mph in less than 3 seconds.

14

It has won three world championships in superbike racing.

The seat, fuel tank, and footrests all move so the rider can make it more comfortable.

# MV Agusta F4 SPR Senna

Ayrton Senna was a famous Formula One racing driver. He died in a race. The Senna motorcycle is named after him.

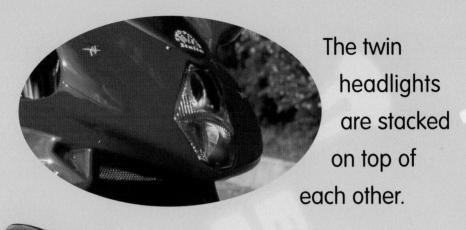

The twin
headlights
are stacked
on top of
each other.

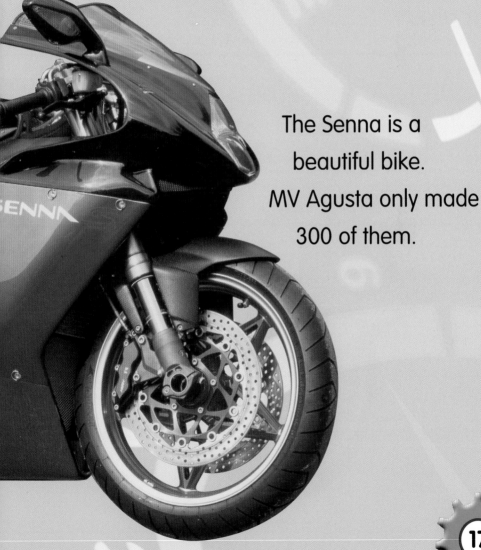

The Senna is a
beautiful bike.
MV Agusta only made
300 of them.

# Suzuki GSX1300R Hayabusa

Suzuki launched the Hayabusa in 1998.
It was the fastest road bike of its time.
A hayabusa is a Japanese bird
of prey.

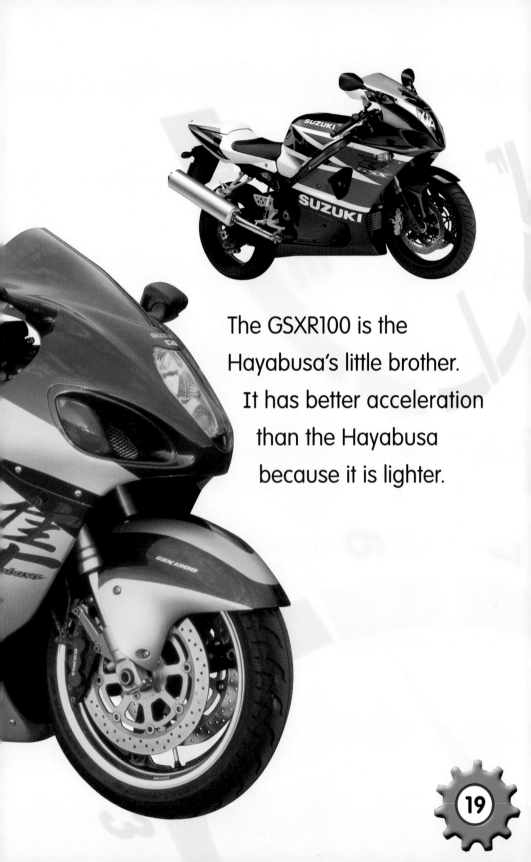

The GSXR100 is the
Hayabusa's little brother.
It has better acceleration
than the Hayabusa
because it is lighter.

# Suzuki GSXR1000

The Suzuki GSXR1000 is a very powerful racing bike. It is used in many superbike world championship races.

Its top speed is 190 mph!

Part of the Suzuki
GSXR1000 is made
of **titanium.** This
makes it so light it
can accelerate from
0 to 60 mph in just under
2.5 seconds.

# Yamaha YZF-R1

Yamaha is famous for making motorcycles. The R1 can do 75 mph in first **gear** and over 99 mph in second gear!

The YZF-R6 is one of Yamaha's most popular bikes. It is small and light but not as fast as an R1.

This is the YZF-R1 2007. It can accelerate from 0 to 60 mph in under 3 seconds. Its top speed is over 188 mph.

# Glossary

| | |
|---|---|
| **accelerate** | To make the bike go faster. |
| **exhaust** | A pipe that takes engine gases away from the rider. |
| **gears** | Toothed wheels used to change the speed of a bike. |
| **streamlined** | A smooth shape that cuts through wind and helps a bike go faster. |
| **titanium** | A very hard, but very light metal. |
| **turbo-charged** | When air is forced into the engine, dragging in fuel for more power. |

# Index